FIRE ROAD

FIRE ROAD

poems

Barbara Siegel Carlson

Dream Horse Press
Aptos, California

Dream Horse Press
Post Office Box 2080, Aptos, California 95001-2080

Fire Road Copyright © 2013 Barbara Siegel Carlson
All rights reserved

Printed in the United States of America
Published in 2013 by Dream Horse Press

ISBN 978-1-935716-24-2

Cover artwork:

Hollywood
by Michael Foulkrod,

michaelfoulkrod.blogspot.com/

In Memory of Morris Siegel
(1925-2013)

CONTENTS

I.

II.

III.

I

My heart has left its dwelling place
And can return no more.

—John Clare

WHO SPEAKS

You can hear the mourning dove call
from a distance. It says what I cannot
understand.

Like the bird on the pavement
whose head was a hollow ruby.

IMPOSSIBLE POEM

This poem has no words to tell you
how it dreams itself off the page
and out of this book because
the page is already erased, and the book
is blank. Just as the room has no walls
to hold me here, the breathing inside
expands to the breathing outside, to the blind
voices of the crickets that keep resounding
through the lightest rain, their nests
always hidden, as the room you've filled
with books written in a language
you never speak out loud, only those words
are not silent but of the night urgent
with messages unsent. I am trying to hear you
sealed in my memory—there was a milk box
by the porch, but it rusted out the bottom,
and the key slipped away. There's this
trapdoor at the back of my throat you keep
falling through. I imagine you mute
in my subterranean heart looking up
from its crevasse to where this poem
is being devoured, even as it rises to the night
teeming with wings drawn like hieroglyphics,
but it's really the whirring that seems to cast
every second into another life. I can't tell
anymore the imagined from the vanished.

THE METAPHYSICS OF GRAMMAR

The preposition directs you to the hour
or place always in between, moving but still,
so you may never arrive. Without the noun
neither you nor I would exist. Maybe a linking
verb is the best state. Look at the rabbit
who spends its life hopping across the wire floor
of a hutch. Waiting. For what? When you sit in a theater
for two hours staring at a movie screen, someone else's
story unreeling before your eyes, are you active
or linking? You need a real verb to sleep well.
Before and after you a sprinkle...you're here...
Or smooth skin...the petal crinkles. A dash
is more abrupt— clumps of hair on your pillow—
an empty side. Never use a period on yourself,
only commas to mark a change of jobs, homes,
friends, spouses, lovers or health. One day
you wake up to a semi-colon where a comma
had been; the neighborhood's grown strange
as you trip on the uneven sidewalk, moss
growing through your soles. A colon brings
a revelation: look in the mirror: your eyes meet.
Another self slips away, which is why
you might find the indefinite pronoun your friend,
the one you turn to when no one is there.

PERSONAL

(after C.D. Wright)

Some mornings my hair looks like sea smoke,
and the drawstring in my nightgown disappears.
I was told in a dream that I was speaking
Etruscan. If you want to find me when I walk
go to the island in the swamp. If we meet
we can share a good smoke on the footbridge.
I still use my manual typewriter
to plunk out dirty letters on onion skin
to strangers like you. Route 44's my own
private runway. One time a sparrow smacked
into my windshield and I left the stain for weeks
till the rain washed it off. I like watching
the number zero appear on the odometer,
the clouds float like grease, and slow dancing
tight. Favorite words: w(hole), ravel, ravish,
and universe, for everyone's a Janus.
It's impossible to see your real face.
I refuse to eat tongue, chopped liver
or lamb. Still have the fake opal earring
stolen for my secret box. My only trophy
for miniature golf, my first place ribbon for the rope
climbing contest; my raffle ticket won me
a *Thing Maker*, a hot plate with molds to make
a creature out of goop. Then you stuck a pencil
through the body. I, too, wore the dead
lady's coat. My nicknames Cream Soda
and Swivel Hips. I spelled it Tim Buck Too.
Once I went sledding down the cellar stairs

on a gate. Another time left a piano in the rain.
Dreamt I was carrying a bird-baby
in my pouch. I'm a great parallel parker but also
write letters while driving. Buried in me is
Elsa the Lion, the silent siren in the mangrove.

MODIGLIANI'S CELLIST

He plays to the violet walls,
to the window's curly brown shadows
and to the mirror that looks on.

Colors that slide down the walls
murky and shapeless.

Is it a reverie or a sob—?
On this warm night
someone has made him feel tender, brutal.

As the bow's hot quiver
cracks through the wood—

BLUE STAIN

I played with my mother's hands
as she read to me. As the blue dot on her arm
lay still, I kept wanting to hear
how the boy stabbed her with a pen
and the ink sunk in and stayed. As the whistle
of a train tore through the bedroom window,
blankets of crickets thickened and bees shivered alive
between the windows. Years later a homeless man
spread a dirty comforter on the pavement below.
In the hum of the violet wires I whispered to him
who could not hear me. Who remembers picking up
a dead bee—the sting that reverberates?
When the El roars over everyone vibrates.
In every wake chimes shudder while a man
clings to his dark secret smell—his mouth
half-open. My mother's blood fills my heart.
The sidewalk heaved up as though
it longed for what she couldn't say.

THE TRUTH

Spinoza is rubbing my glasses again, leaving
the middle range blurred for a reason.
Any truth is a blur. I can write at the same time
as I peel an orange. This is a trick
my grandfather taught me: to peel the skin to a swirl
and place your fist inside. Then smell your hand
like the river out the window whose lull
is a blur in the wind. Who
holds the truth? My friend drank some white lightning
till it electrified his veins. This is how simple it is
to become a street person.
When Father Charlie asked for prayers
the homeless man said Jesus fished out his soul.
I shook his hand. Later he covered his face
with his hands and laid his head in his lap. We all have
missing teeth, holes where other teeth still try
to grow, button holes that look lonely and pillowcases
that tear to let the feathers out. My friend had a daughter
who didn't know she was his daughter.
This is the truth, the only truth he could ever live with
for that moment that has lasted
her whole life. I was given a portrait
of many galaxies spinning among the dwarves.
Spinoza must have known the hottest colors
came from the stars in his hands. We have no age.
Before the Big Bang we were swimming
through each other. A spider draws from a bottomless self
raveling its meal into the lightest being,

as Miro painted *Rosalie sleeping in a web*
washed by the dew that fell from a bird wing.
Each strand of the truth has an unknown emanation.
In Chekhov's story the student wept
for the two peasant women listening to a simple retelling
of Jesus's message to Peter about his betrayal.
An ancient pain, a thread
in the wooden footbridge I used to cross
with my thick-tired bike as I passed through the chain
of smokers, too shy to look up. Once a girl named Diane
blew smoke in my face.

A HAUNTING MUSIC

There is nothing but a spiritual world.

— *Kafka*

In a needlepoint you named the Ninevah Gardens
I saw only faint lines, the curve
of your hand underneath.
The raindrops are all connected
like embroidery thread on the other side.
People in Pliny's time believed
we were born from the dew.
Each November all the abandoned nests
become visible. The seagull is screaming
but no sound comes out. Why
is the smallest particle called God?
My grandfather remembered the ringing
of the bells before every pogrom.
After he went deaf the bells kept ringing.

THIRST TAKES MANY FORMS

An iceberg 6 times the size of Manhattan has just broken free.
Radioactive boars are running around parts of Germany.
In the library parking lot you pick up a clear
plastic leaf the size of a thumbnail. It gleams like the silver
wheels of teeth around the well drilling place. Where's the light
when you point at an empty spot in the galaxy?
Your eyes reflect those myriads opening into a prayer
like sex—a deer that can smell water from miles away.
Why did the Native woman believe her soap could lift a tumor
like a small rock out of a man's cheek? The fence section
encloses nothing. Do you hear the soul creeping upstairs?
How can you kiss the mind of the one who threw a flaming wad of
toilet tissue into the stall where a black girl sat— you, flames
of the heart licking through—Boy, why did you let go of the other
boy's hand before he dove into the quarry? Who dreams
out your eyes? A shopping cart lies at the bottom.

INVISIBLE BORDER

Somewhere in Hungary
a boxcar stands in a field.

A purple stain on the floor
where a little straw is strewn.

All around is the desolate
field, no one. Vibrating trains

all around. No one stops.
Under fast moving clouds

the roar of the wind, a stream
of sun through the slats –

no one stops.

IOWA RIVER

(after Gerald Stern)

This is where I held my words,
by the rising water, along the brick buildings.
I sat there listening, mumbling to myself,
quivering a little. I was thirsty at best,
pretending to be strong, trying to be free
without letting go. This is how I looked
at the message in my hand, the river
overflowing the sides, one arm shaking, one arm
sweating. That is the airplane
and those are the sparrows; when it lands
the rumbling is only birdsong, a silence
here and there, some droning to live by.
That is my footprint and here is my flashlight
beaming through the leaves; those are
the fireflies blinking in and out, and that is the waterfall
crashing. I am standing up. I think a bear
clawed my forehead. I have a hook
at the end of my nose and a wart by my eyebrow.
The water is thick and savage under the bridge; one color
has so many shades—overwhelming
except for the moment; one word leaks
like a strand; almost clear, it throbs
and glitters, it rushes with passion, it weeps with fading.
It is the most quiet alive. A raving.

WITHOUT TOUCHING

Sunlight warms my knees. We used to play statue
on the lawn after supper. A fly taps the glass.
"Money is everything," Uncle Ben once said.
In the Jewish Cemetery slabs lean in every direction.
It's impossible to see each other without touching
a chandelier of human bones. You tap
the glass. Do you remember the gypsy girl
selling binoculars? "Money is everything," preached
Uncle Ben. Sunlight taps the glass. We played
we were statues on the lawn after supper. The earth's a blue
dot that holds all love and strife. It's impossible
to see each other without touching. Do you remember
the gypsy girl's cracked lip? We whirled and then fell
on the lawn after supper. Human rocks
under a waving branch. The swirling aches.
Sun like a knife through the open door.

ABANDONED HOUSE

Out on the porch
the screen filled with pearls.

Webs of dead flies breathe
in the corners.

When a train passes by
the spiders cry out.

She forgot where she hid the key.

ON DOORS

The door itself has no door.
But it opens to another door.
A keyhole blazes before you.

A door made of a pigeon wing.
In the palm you cannot see through.
Doors are locked even when they're open.

How can you open a door you can't see?
The heart of the door does not ache.
Darkness is a door that opens both ways.

The anxious knock of a lover,
the desperate knock of the pursued,
the hesitant knock of the estranged.

Souls pass through doors.
Stand between the double doors
where they whisper your name.

SHADOW CROSSING

A shadow is crossing the plain. It glides
over a concrete tower that looks like a torch,
a tree cracked in half near some yellow flowers.
Just past an abandoned building
swarming in graffiti. Passing
a pile of blankets, a car with no hood.

Two gypsy women walk along the track.
One swishes her long colorful skirt.
The other has dark mournful eyes
that look up just as the shadow passes.
We pass a boy with a huge head
throwing a stick to his dog, and the dog
never stops running.

Someone has written *Look in*
on the side of a house. Impossible to see
through any window. One window appears
filled with fire: someone is burning inside,
drinking, lying down, saying nothing.
The sunflowers' lolling heads bow
to their shadows that have no face or color.
Fear grips me again.

LANGUAGE LESSON

Lidice, Czech Republic

What is your name?
A word, a mouthful of wind.

Where are you from?
The top layer of dust and the chain's rustle.

What's your profession?
Like the subject of your sentence that has no ending
or darkness pouring through an upstairs window.

Where did you go to school?
By a farmhouse no longer there.

Where is it? Beside bones smooth as birch wood,
blent into the hairs that line the burrows of moles.

How old are you?
Older than the forest of flesh, younger than the mud
of lost infants. They tried to cast me into bronze
with the others. But I swayed. I got away.

Where did you go?
Into a bed smoking to the sky and the pail I drank milk from
that melted into a clump.

Where do you live now?
In the questions that breathe from our lost mouths.
In the words that are animals following a scent through vibrations,
only they make the forest lonely.

Where is the forest?
It's invisible, the roots are still there, they made hail
across the wheat never harvested. Because the water
froze inside our burning veins.

What is the word for a burning vein?
The silence you light with your lips.

The Czech village of Lidice was destroyed by the Nazis in 1942 in retaliation for the assassination of SS leader Reinhard Heydrich.

II

Do not throw away
Shoes with holes, through them
You can see the path better.

— Luko Paljetak (Croatia, b. 1943)

THE OTHER ROAD

The road has no destination.
My little history is zero.
My blank book called The Argument.
I am in love with the other road.
People are born without names.
Birds hatch under the glass roof,
snatch seeds from my hand.
I am opened by the orange beak of a swan.
The burning waves and heaves.
What the dead teach.
That the box with no flaps sighs
as it collapses. That the mattress exudes
septic crumbs, viruses and abbreviations
that tick, tick through spring.
In May the fans rattle. Luscious leaves
are filled with grace. The trees sweat
green winds. Lovesickness thrives,
spinning blades without longing.
It is born into the waves of longing
to erase us, spread us. To be more
than our skeletal lives, our bereft thinking.
Zeus thrust into my soul. My eyes broke
like glass through the aviary. I saw the last
dusky seaside sparrow in its jar on the shelf.
A white soul dove into the road to cover me.
I lay like salt on the burning road.

MEETING

He said he ate a porcupine raw.
She said she heard the clouds speak her name.
He said there were winters the roads
were never touched. She said if you spoke back
the sun would slit open your skin.
He said bones have a secret meat. She said here,
take this white pear and green pear
that I cradle in my red coat, I have many
that look like stones, like eggs, like eyes.
He said the word marrow rhymes
with arrow. She said I ate my own sorrow,
my own ambrosia I licked from the bark,
my blood knows your speech. He said
there are worms in every square inch
we can't see. She said then how can you know
what you hold, who you are, where you burn
in your quiver of souls, your urn of children,
your oven of honeysuckle.

TREATISE ON THE WHISPER

I think about whispers and how one
blushed red as sumac. Now it's
lying just outside your door.
The rain comes clattering down
the street in Berlin where you whispered
you lived across from the sex shop.
Many whispers rubbed against each other,
crossed curbs and gathered over thresholds,
the cobbles kept none. I'd like to be the needle
whispering to the thread, the blue one
in your arm. Then there'd be no more terrorists
where the doors wouldn't lock.
I read about a man who survived 27 days
under the rubble of a whisper.
A whisper licking a woman's lips kept her alive.
Whispers live in our fingers,
tapping away. Another saw her own whisper
slip out as three. She believed one of them
could charm the snakes in her soul.
Some whispers are dipped in tar. Their feet grieve.
They called me Seagull as if I could taste
the salt of a distant whisper.
Some are words I can't say out loud.
A whisper leaks many hungers.
My tongue can't stop the whisper.
They stain my belly. Berries ripen
around them dropping slowly. A red tailed hawk
screeches over in widening arcs, its feathers blush
in the dying sun and silence shakes over everything.

LEAVING A HOLLOW

When you enter me I grow invisible
like one of those sea creatures
in the middle waters, the black medusa
that sucks in its own light and so
seems to vanish. What if this universe
swallows our souls as we wait
for another wakefulness?
Thoreau wrote about a worm
that emerged from a knot after a hundred years
leaving a hollow at the heart.
What we live on can never be told.

MIGRANTS

As I ride by the cranberry bog I glance at the small group in
wide-brimmed hats and baggy pants bending over and weeding.
Everyone's veiled in fog. A milky sun coming up. Perhaps they've
been standing there a couple hours already. One of the women
pauses to look at her hand. Maybe it's sore. Maybe her shoulder
aches, and she's thinking of her child being cared for by her
sister who is sad because she's far away from her child. In fact,
so far away she never even knew her child, had to give him up
because she was too young. Now she's taking care of someone
else's. One day I saw a small girl in a car parked near the bog. She
was coloring in a book. As I walked by I smiled and waved.
For a moment she looked at me, then back down. We're all on
our way somewhere.

AUTOBIOGRAPHY

I step onto the train with a suitcase of books
written in a language I can't speak.
The train won't stop
in my childhood town.

I remember my cat walking by
a lit candle. The train blazes through
colored trees, a charred pile
where the hotel shaped like a ship
burned down. There's still a sign
for Native American trinkets.

Once my parents bought me a head-dress
of the brightest feathers. A gust
blew my head-dress into the sea.

Shivering in my blue seat
in the middle of the flames, I pass
my father walking backwards and
I call to him in a lit whisper.

DOG WITH NO WINGS

I want to walk through people's hearts.

—*Srečko Kosovel*

My neighbor is hanging her sheets and husband's t-shirts
on the line. What does she whisper to herself on this bright
morning after rain? A torn Queen Anne chair waits across
the road to be taken. What family secret leaks through
the cushions? What about the Madonna in the bathtub
stained with exhaust, staring beyond whoever passes?

A boy draws up a shade as I walk by a bag of books with
no jackets. It's trash day. Around the corner a statue of
an angel has a hole in its back. I never meant to betray you,
says one of its crumpled up tissues inside. Everything's wet,
bindings unglued. I rock my dark soul under a cloud.
Yesterday a woman heaved herself into a river with
her unborn child. Where can I place them in this poem?

I glance at the roadside silt, the sweepings of pine needles.
Is it like reading tea leaves—the heart? My feet map a route
no one will ever see. Hardy's heart was cut out of his chest.
A dog with no wings lies on the shoulder, unclaimed.

For centuries Copernicus lay hidden under a cathedral.
Where does the truth of any love go? The puddles look
like openings into the unattainable. At home my mirror
faces a wall. From whose cord was love cut?

AFTER THE SUICIDE OF A FRIEND

At the funeral luncheon a bouquet quivered.
Someone shook my hand. A painting
trembled out of its frame when the coal truck rumbled by.
One of the mirrors cracked. I pulled a caterpillar
from my hair and the juice trickled
all over my hand. I walk past a boarded-up house.
Missing stairs. Weeds flutter outside the rotten frames.
I keep wishing I could see through walls, learn
what happens in my narrow room. All night
the coal trucks rumble by, and the miners punch in.
As the red lights bleed from wall to wall, shells
shatter on a distant beach. Over pot holes
the driver keeps lurching, bottomless as his sagging bed.
When the lonely feel desperate the roads rattle
like sheets on a windy line. Hearts are leaking out
whose walls reek with secret flowers that keep sprouting
in the dark. There's a cave in southern Maryland
where crystals have blossomed for millions of years
in a vacuum. Then someone broke through the wall,
and now the whole ceiling glitters with petrified spiders,
while hundreds of fathoms deep the miners pray over coals
of hope, and I'm trapped between the shuddering
limbs of one love while another unravels on its own.
Every bed streams under the springs. Aren't we all flies
wrapped in silk? Unbearably light to be carried and strewn
like butterflies rising in the wake of a truck. For a moment
the cinders shine. Then a gust flings open the door—

BEAST'S LULLABY

After you left I waited in the mansion, shedding
like a dog. Humming to my flower till nothing came out.
The kitchen mat throbbing. Wings crushed inside my shoulders
rustled the oven door, and the bile broke out. Silverfish streamed
out my story. They slithered over my Orpheus, my lava.
They tasted Schubert's lips. Slipped down the vines
like spineless violins. I was drunk along the highway, rubbing the fur
that clung to the bones of trees. Your brilliant needle
kissed me once. Punctured my drums into thickets of blood.
Rain hammering on my twenty nails of loneliness. Who can hear
the rose cry through its body of thorns? The mosses all harden,
the starlings' dirges stuffed with earwigs. What oozes
from the infernal clouds? I drank the black drops of such living things.
Felt a quiver roar up my fur. A machine gun pointed at my heart.
My slobbering deer, messengers of the gods—they were the crooners,
the whimperers that gurgled in my chest, roiling my soul's mercy.
I couldn't follow a firefly. Couldn't swallow the aurora borealis
that tore through me. Was I your hare-lip? Your lost Holderlin?
Maybe I ravaged my own silence and called it love. Your petals
bleed around a monstrous ache. Spit it out, you'd say, this acrid pipe
buried like a song-bone. Maybe my eye was gouged out of a billboard's
face and floats down the smoggy river, through the ashen woods.
Maybe Orpheus wept when the night birds found my heart.

HERMIONE REVISED

I heard a rustle a click   my father said
nothing the others looked down
Later I swallowed bugs   mouthfuls
of sand longing for the horizon
to take me   to her I tried to touch
its gleaming edge he dragged me back opened
his needle eye the violet thread   between sea and sky
feathers of spume   the moon cold-
eye   looking for me   my mouth a devil's cradle
rocking the blue worm the rank
weeds called witch's hair   my lips stung
memory is moldy and reeks rocks melike a mockingbird
deadinacrack
my mouth   is a ravenous sin a black sun   imploding
torn from a red-hot tongue   under wings my burning ring
summer lightning lit open the sky
rock-a-bye mute mother your broken branch   the truth
scratched from the myth   and shame handed down
endlessly rocking waves   tear a body down

Hermione is the daughter of Helen of Troy

IN BATTONYA, HUNGARY

Easily
your womb opened up, softly
a breath rose into the air
and what turned to cloud—wasn't it
wasn't it a shape of our own making…
—Paul Celan

Smell of wet smoke, juicy breath of sheep and goats
in old wooden folds, damp cupboards, overripe fruits
and root vegetables—all the spices rising
like yeast. A chorus of dogs and watery rooster cries
wanders over the roofs. The howling feels vast—half-rhapsodic,
half-lamentable spillage of secrets and dreams gathered
and released from time's lost waves. From a nearby yard
comes a shrill voice, then a door scrapes open.
One of the peacocks shrieks. Sounds of living rouse
all around—bicycles wheels whirring by, the rush
of a car motor in a village of few cars, running water,
ring of a heavy pot, clang of a dish, thunk of a knife
on a cutting board. What is it that can't be heard?
Who murmurs…? What pulp of song's black seed, raw
with an odor of ravines and deep bruised bodies
of clouds seeping down, stirring on the other side of the wall
a bed to groan, and reverberations from the iron bells…
whose animal yearning lets go to this fume of cat pee
and rotting plum, musky fur, sweat and refuse?
Hear them breathe, smell the brine, the moist wind
on the heavy leaves rocking each limb with the blood of a lullaby.

NOT KNOWING

Walking down the street one night
I found my heart drifting toward
a young Latino woman with a broken
high heel, the tops of her brown breasts
almost heaved out of her coat.
A newspaper sheet came flying
around the corner and clung
to my shoulder. For a moment I understood
that whatever touched me
was nothing I could ever grasp.
I passed a long line of men waiting
for their plates of lamb.
How the sidewalk trembled
under those men who stood quiet
and waited, some steam
from the pavement grate rose.
We all breathed waiting to be filled
as the wind tore down the avenue
not knowing what it thirsted for.

HAGAR

At first he ran ahead scrambling up the rocky ledges bragging
he could climb all day. He poked at a lamb bone. Now
we stumble toward a glittering edge that never vanishes.
I've lost my shadow. Yesterday the desert beckoned pink
as a shell's interior. By noon the air was afire. I can't
close my eyes. A radiance not my own quivers
like the darkness in his loins. Invisible beaks peck
at my lids and my heels—I'm featherless, crave
the waters of darkness. My son and I blind
to the future. Now it's a blanket of pain only the sun
drizzles through. The moon lifts a ghostly
fingertip into the void. How can the days hold love? Cast out
to embrace what swells, then withers my cheeks. Bruises
the bleached rocks. The horizon's blushed milk. My love
whose heat bears the blue flame of God I too taste like the sea
that was burning between my legs, and whose wick
lighted me before her. I'm swollen with stings and the sparks
that split open my heart. What can I say to my own betrayal?
Whose coals blaze before us? Who will find us? We're too
far away to hear whatever you utter and so let go.
You come to me in sleep. Your voice breaks me.
Where do we go? I taste the iron and salt of the dead
that you rubbed into my womb. Can't breathe beneath
your gaze or flutter out your throat. My body keeps trembling,
rocking you of no shadow who filled me with lightness and dew.

IN A BURIED KEY

Under Ljubljana's Dragon Bridge a red-eyed man sits
collecting coins and handing out tickets for the toilet.
What does he care if the medieval bells jangle?
An old gypsy woman climbs up the stairs in a soiled coat
and pink sneakers, wanders from table to table
along the river: *O poorah, sanjam*...she wails
to each customer, her eyes the color of silt, her mouth
holds a thick tongue. In between cries a child
inconsolable, unraveling past the sculpture
of the faceless man with a tail that guards
Butcher's Bridge and its padlocks hanging along
the rail as if love can be sealed with a click
if you bury the key. But lives have pried loose—
in these cries ringing out past the statue of Prometheus
with the eagle at his gut, brushing out the stricken eyes.
At an empty table a sparrow opens its red throat,
but no sound comes out. All that survives
of Giotto's "Shipwreck" are two angel heads
from the frame. What cries they wrenched free.

THE EMPTY STRETCHES

What stays in the desolate places
along the interstate between the corridors
of wind? What's left that's fresh
as the smell of rain on asphalt
from the charcoal-streaked fingers of clouds
that drench the stubble fields?
Those jagged peaks in the distance steeped
with day and night—even as their edges
lift away, their ridges tinged yellowy-violet
as an old bruise. Beneath wind, water and sun, exposed
to all who pass and then are gone, alone
with the blazing and bone-clear nights
when stars pass through the soul
as they that were heaved up
and carved wear back into blackness.
What do their shadows cast? Where no one lives
runs clear and rough over this
bare road that carries us.

III

In the movement of its wings there lingered the same faith that the body's unrest can raise a wind carrying us to longed-for worlds.

—Zbigniew Herbert

UNSPOKEN SPEECH

for a stillborn

She holds a jar of smoke. Spins around a black scribble.
It's a spoon with ears of butter, a cry seeking a music box.
Sculpted out of moonstones and wild powders, lovesick
from the wind. Her self-portrait found in a blind man's eye.
Why won't her limbs stop shaking? They trace the ivy of
the black light, the blood of cinders and sinners. Sighs
from the writhing vine. Someone baked a piece of paper with her
name written all over it. Music breaking up like her mind.
She's lit with the madness of a murderer and the sorrow
of a harlot. Rattling strings as the lyrics of this strange fruit
tear her apart. Who sleeps in the vapors of passion?
Every undulation and tendril possess her. Every fold and seam
becoming hairs falling from the sun. The brush of this black fur
radiates. What dancing snakes. Everyone's drama's a dream,
a pin cushion of enigmas. Internal organs laid bare. Behind the curtain
her drunk lover yelling for food. An ant, a dog and a beggar
share one shadow. Her soul's green flame is ablaze in the bed.
Still the burning bush, the ashes she rubs like a lamp.

WHEN YOU CAN'T FILL IN THE BLANK

Weather is a fruit fly. The heart bounces
out of a broken shell. Through the bus
comes the crunch of a fortune cookie.
After awhile, conversations grow sweaty.
Chimes tinkled under the falling hairs.
I don't know how long Tillie was staring
at the pillar on Elmora Ave. A shadow
striking the windshield, between bars without a tune.
The chimes didn't tinkle—they were under a spell.
How do you spell nothing with no letters?
Under every tongue dances zoyzia grass.
Since the number 4 & the word 'death' are the same
in Chinese, the people refuse to eat liver.
"Emotions are streets." I feel for blind spots.
The striped pajamas of history keep flickering.
A mermaid painted on an abandoned
brick building among the oil refineries. Someone
changed the rules of the curtain. She went on a date
with a cylinder to swim the power lines. Babs never did
figure out how to use the slide ruler. There will be a war
between metal detectors in the parking lot.
She clung to the lily of the valley smell
in the latrine. Then a permanent tissue blushed
at the sight of a verandah. The dead end is always
a live wire. *Oy gevalt.* I was riding the waves
of the siren with no arms. The sisters Malaria
and Melanoma kept laughing after the show ended.
Between lanes on the interstate, a lost ball.

NEAR THE RODEWAY INN

Monterey, California

Maybe because stone lions are guarding
the entrance to Chef Lee's Mandarin House
in the early morning fog,
you can sip your coffee in solitude
on the ledge that overlooks
a jade garden made to look like an oasis
by the highway—

That lagoon in the middle,
its craggy hill with a hole
in the top for the water. And those steps
cut into the mountain
that will never be climbed.

Maybe they trace another route
to the islands of clouds you keep driving toward
or the soul you keep reaching for
as it passes through worlds

like the red-gold dragon on the roof breathing out
its flame of clay, or the crow drinking
from a puddle that, for a moment, glows
in the parking lot beyond.

WAKING ALONE

I'm wearing the lacy top a woman crippled
with arthritis stitched. Some nights I wake up
to the ecstatic cries of coyotes. Every rootless love
stretches across winds carried by dragonflies.
My own sap trickles. In all directions
are ladders without rungs. A firefly lights
its own way. I sleep alone. Wake
to the half-dead oak. Reach for someone
not there—at the most ravenous point
memory goes blind, while the roots crawl
pushing through sand and clay like a needle
through heavy fabric. Shrill resonance of crickets
whose wings ignite dreams that make holes
in the dense dark of my own unknown country.

KAFKA

Two o'clock on his way home. Sun beats
down his neck. He takes a different route.
Pigeons gurgling from a ledge as though calling
Franz, Franz, your dinner is ready!
It's the voice of his old nurse
who gave him oatmeal in bed and told him
the story of a man whose back was scarred
with a map of a city. A building's
on fire—walls rise
to the sky. For a moment a human figure
at one of the windows ripples
into a soundless plume.

DRAMATIS PERSONAE

If this is a poem it has no words.
If it's made of words it can't be touched.
If it's made to be touched
it can't be a poem.

If this is a poem it releases a fly.
If the fly can't be seen
it has buzzed out your ear.
If it lands on your hand it will reek of your heart.

If this is a poem it tells no lies.
It repeats your story but can't be true.
If it hides on the page
it will steal your obsessions.

If this is a poem it follows no lines.
If it draws one line it will draw another.
If the line makes you twitch
it will be your burden.

If this is a poem it breathes with knives,
it kisses with torches
and dreams with shards.
If this is a poem it spins on empty.

If this is a poem it imagines your death.
If death loves your song it won't tell why.
If your song does not die
you will have no bed.

If this is a poem it will taste of your love.
If love is bitter the blood is sweet.
If your hand is lonely
a fly will come.

If this is a poem it is only words.
If the words make you mute your soul will be fed.
If your soul is not hungry
the poem will be dead.

ABOUT THE AUTHOR

AZ was born in an elevator. She's the ghost author
of the *Inchworm Series, The Anachronistic Fisherwoman*
and a collection of matchbooks in Esperanto.
Grants from Verbatim International to Verboten Express
hang on the wall. So many pins have been issued to her
she can't maintain them due to insufficient security.
Prizes include the No Name Award, The Brightest Cryptic
and Fugitive's Choice. She's received advances from
A Random Press as well as candy ants for her driftwood
lover's anthology. *Greatest Shadows* is forthcoming
made after nights of loving (or longing—she can't
remember which). From her ex she kept the rain-stick
and glass flute. She lights many candles and sings
each night by running her hand over them
till the melody turns to a scream. When she draws up
the shade the shadows look like bodies strewn
on a battlefield. She slips down the stairs, out the side door
and enters her grandmother's house, climbs
to the attic and touches the cheek of the first face
she saw in a coffin, that of her dark cleaning woman
who had been beaten by her husband. The cheek
smooth as moonstone, and she hovers there
for a long time, afraid to wash her hand of the pain.

I CANNOT SAY

Skocjan, Slovenia

"...if we lose our ruins we will be left with nothing..."
—*Zbigniew Herbert*

River of rushing
holes in stone
under moss the hollows grow
wet, my insides
wet as the green slabs
I want to sleep with the green
oily secrets, arms
legs of the living language spreading
under the fort ruins
black as the cave's mouth
Who goes with you, after you?
Rises and falls
along ghostly lines
crumbled soul
alive by the molten flickers
you'll never be skin, petals of blood
your bone, your country
will never be found
I want to stay
lick the roots of time
under the dead leaves
the woods unheard
no water for this
unknown inside
word I cannot say
remains—I want to leave

myself with the blackness, the moss
that covers the rocks and roots—
killer with a voice
where there isn't any

TIERGARTEN

Paths wind through the park's thick undergrowth.
Rainbows shimmer above the sprinklers and white
shadows of leaves, then the sunlight hardened
into a glaze of stone eyes as those of the Kaiser
gazing across the pond at his marble Luisa.
Through a chain of purplish trees I had come
to the bus stop among the fresh fumes of passing cars.
Sunlight hit the sign and the words faint
noting the villa where the organization to
'annihilate worthless life' began. There was
no ark, only the dark madness underneath.
Across the bridge beneath the shining pond under
a cloudless sky, the silence pressed down.
The pavement glittered without water.
Past the dripping roses, swallows and larks
swooping down to the roots and hoses all tangled
before a small meadow, the steel gate locked.
It was a hunter's paradise—all of Berlin mourned
when Luisa died. A hundred years later when
the patients were led out of the asylums to
their deaths, was the rain dark drumming down
or did it light their faces? Told they were being saved,
did they believe themselves blessed? It's summer.
A man in a white suit looks up at a tree of falling dew.
Everything is lush, hushed, the sprinklers come on
and water the empty walks. One of the branches shakes.

DEATH SONG

In the grass and the greenness, the blades
and the roots, and in the earth surrounding them;
in the water and my fear of the water.
In the black trunk the red sap oozing out. In every
inch of my skin, every drop of sweat, my scent
like a scar, my tears with their memories, the heat
of my whisper. In each one what peeled away,
what hair I shed and did not shed. In each blind spot
what breathes. In my saliva of brine sour
as a stalk. In the face I cannot see,
in the voice unheard, in the body
I can't touch—there's a stump out my window, a vine
hanging down, a frayed piece of rope
where a swing once rocked that doesn't stop.

LITTER

Every day I walk along the road looking down
at the random things as though they've washed up
on some beach: strips of a tire, a broken mirror,
crumpled McDonalds wrappers, gum wrappers,
peanut shells, cigarette filters that exploded
in the rain, smashed soda and beer cans, more broken
glass, rusty screws, a condom, and then there are
the small animals, like today a mouse-like creature
lying in the gray sand—almost a silhouette, but
it still shakes me a little now that it's just a thing
lying there in the grit among a few twigs,
a used lottery ticket. For a moment I hover
over it, its pin hole eye. I've left no tracks.
I carry nothing in my hands. I move away.

TO THE BLANK PAGE

Were you a mistake in the middle
of the book of old maps
I found under my bed--? "Highways Unseen,"
"Lost in the Lilies," "Cartographer's Breath
on a Cold Day," "Static," "Dead Space," "O Great
Unknowable." I scratch too hard
and tear through the sheet.

Once a pigeon left crumbs
in my bed, trails that lost their way.
My head sinks into a pillow,
while my mind flees. Maybe it spews
to the clouds, something radiant
that showers back down with a blinding pitch.

A god's hair lights up the oven of time.
My mother's memory was delivered
to you. My father's blood
leaks where my sister's speech falters.
Sweet land of liberty. Holy wafers melt down
your throat as love withers on a twig
and the dead dissolve
between roots and stones.
Your heart's white forest absorbs all this,
thins to a shuddering leaf...

No one walks on water or writes in smoke.
But colors sprout underneath

like the sex of the unborn. Streaming clouds
fill your eyes, your mouth.
Do you annihilate dreams or feed them?
Is it the blood of centuries
that stokes you to this clarity? Your limestone bed
will be sucked down a sink hole.

You've been erased—every word, every name
blazes down this fire road the maps
leave out. Here is a body
unearthed. Spectral bones like the gold sweat
lame Vulcan found in a fisherman's coal.
Who of this trackless land kisses the sky?
Whose hunger breaks open the bud?

NOT THERE YET

a battlefield near Staunton, Virginia

Two blackbirds perch themselves on opposite poles.
Deep wounds fill in the pasture. The wind washes
your face. So much silence is buried here. So much
love and pain. One of the birds takes off. I watch
its powerful wings wondering where it will land next
and what it will take. We both watch as a kind
of distraction. What we don't know remains. What we
leave and touch. Now the sun's ripped through
the clouds blanketing the field with exquisite softness.
All the blades like rivulets of a sad, unheard music.
I cannot say what I know of love or feel where grief
comes from. Once more a cloud covers the sun.
The other bird flies off into a barren landscape.
The wind doesn't know how the body aches.

HIDDEN

What hides in the mass of your sleeping
body next to me? What hides upside down
in the picture in the coloring book
that crumbles in the basement? Or the sigh
of our cat? What hides in the lips of one
ex-lover dreaming on the church floor, holding
the picture of his dead infant on a chain
around his neck? In the mouth
of the man who drew a rat to his lips
before an audience of living statues?
In the soul of the woman in child's pose
on the street, one finger tapping
a paper cup? What hides in the paper
neither of us can read? In the voice
we can't speak? In the memory neither of us
can reach across. In the tooth whose phantom
roots draw from an unfathomable source,
whose layers have no smell, whose breath
has no wisdom, whose poetry has no bread,
but it rises in some child's chest as he strays
out the school door multiplying every day
hidden. It hides where the others mingle,
breathing its dark impossible music.

A LOST WORLD

A toothless man on the T is chewing,
hunched over his cloth satchel
stuffed with plastic bags, empty
seats on both sides.

He keeps on chewing,
his yarmulke shines black and satiny
like the ones kept in a wooden box
outside the sanctuary.

Haunted by prayers and regrets,
the flicker of souls.

Locked in a story or else
locked out of it,
riding a train that never stops,
though the doors are clear,
and people with dreams like mine
keep stepping inside.

AFTER YOU LEFT

1.
After midnight I woke to people
singing below,

then a car door opened
to the orange glow of a cigarette.

You were gone.

Ashes were falling like snow,
they glowed like a curtain
in the wake of a great love.

2.
The bitter smell of old coffee,
an empty bowl,

where to place the pleasures
of the body, its terrible softness
and memories that cling
like a cobweb,

fingerprints that stain the night
pressing deeper into nothingness.

KISS ON THE PAVEMENT

Longing is the wind
just before you got into the car
we grow more and clearly alone
you put your arm around my waist
and the lines we leave
fill with light, the lightness alone
pulled me close, tongue slipped through my lips
as the longing unbroken
fluttered inside my mouth
part-animal, part-human, a knife-star
as it blazed
to break free of itself
never sheathe it with words
never know which part
is the passion, which part the divine
the blade held close

ON DEPARTURES

Near dusk I come to the pond's edge.
The swans splash, dunking
their heads into the black water
of broken ice. Is blindness
black or white? Crystals melt
into my coat, knockings
no one hears and echoes
with unanswerable rings.
Sometimes the ice seems to cry.
The swans don't care
what falls in slivers,
the myriads of blades
that fall off their feathers
and disappear. Dear heart,
the light of dead stars
is full of gusts and grace.

INCOMPLETENESS

The heart is always a remnant.
—*Tess Gallagher*

Kuala Lumpur is the only city
with a forest of monkeys in the middle of it.
The proteus has no eyes
and lives for a hundred years
feeling its way through a labyrinth. Something spreads the branch,
wavers in the brown glass. In the fresco underdrawing.
A red leaf falls, its stem
forever dangles.
What did the angel say to the armless one? How Marco Polo
made us believe
there were humans without heads,
the face in the middle of the body, heart streaming
to see. What did Mozart wake and release
that will never rest, how the language of infinity
enters the dead. While angst echoes
a wail breaks through,
and all the chords tremble.

MORNING WALK

A black dog carries its own leash.
Crates of fresh peaches
are like a wind in the alley. The girl
who bites into a sweet green
licorice snake,
the man in an orange uniform
sweeping dust from a stair, gazing off.
From somewhere a mourning dove
calls. Bodies
brush against each other, our particles
collide. A siren's screaming by.
I'm lured
by the scent of a cut flower, a flame-
colored shirt, cries naked
and mute—Desire, desire keeps howling
past the white dog
that has no leash
and runs in an endless circle.

TENDERNESS

Down the street I found a valentine card
ripped in half, the name missing.
Lint all over the ferns.
In the abandoned lot I touched a bird body
with my shoe. What are these things
that pierce me with longing
as though I were that softness, that brushed aside
tenderness? All the leaves
have blown away leaving my body
alone, my softness
untouched. Me with my heart that is
wild, estranged
from the body that holds it
trapping time so my white skin
covers the black
of the missing. In the abandoned night I can almost
hear you calling
from your dream of feathers
locked elsewhere in sleep.
My heart is buried in yours.
Buried in the ants and crushed gravel,
the rusted barbs and still green
briars. Buried in your larger despair. But
I stay silent, fallen bird, because I know
my soul is eternal, in some other dimension
with the blood and wind
afflicted and unknown.

ACKNOWLEDGMENTS

Grateful acknowledgement is made to the following journals in which these poems first appeared, sometimes in different versions:

Asheville Poetry Review: "Dog with No Wings"

The Café Review: "Kafka," "Morning Walk"

The Carolina Quarterly: "Without Touching"

Connecticut River Review: "Unspoken Speech"

Cutthroat: "Meeting" "Beast's Lullaby," "Treatise on the Whisper," "The Other Road" and "Iowa River"

Lake Effect: "The Metaphysics of Grammar" and "Leaving a Hollow"

The Louisville Review: "To the Blank Page" ("Blank Page")

NOR: "Migrants" and "Shadow Crossing"

The Ocean State Review: "Blue Stain"

Poetry Miscellany: "Personal," "Impossible Poem," "The Truth," and "When You Can't Fill in the Blank"

Poetry Porch (http://www.poetryporch.com): "Autobiography," "A Haunting Music," "On Doors"

I am grateful for the friends who have kept me going and helped me with their suggestions through the years, especially Ana Jelnikar, Judy Chalmer, Tam Neville, Nancy Logomarsina, Dzvinia Orlowsky, Scott Withiam, Barbara Korun, Meta Kusar, Moira Linehan and Deborah Brown. Special thanks to the Vermont College of Fine Arts writing community, especially Richard Jackson, for his invaluable responses and belief in my work; Pattianne Rogers and the late Lynda Hull. Thank you, Barbara Buettner for first inspiring me. I am indebted to J.P. Dancing Bear for making this book possible. Finally, to my family I owe countless thanks.

Biography:

Barbara Siegel Carlson grew up in Cranford, New Jersey. She is a graduate of University of Rhode Island and the Vermont College of Fine Arts MFA Program. She is co-translator, with Ana Jelnikar, of *Look Back, Look Ahead Selected Poems of Srečko Kosovel* and the author of the chapbook *Between this Quivering*. Her poems and translations have appeared in *NOR (New Ohio Review)*, *The Carolina Quarterly, Asheville Poetry Review, The Literary Review, Mid-American Review, Cutthroat, Prairie Schooner, Agni* and elsewhere. She lives in Carver, Massachusetts.